D1433107

Cooking *for all* OCCASIONS

Wendy Veale

MARTIN BOOKS

Published by Martin Books
Simon & Schuster Consumer Group
Grafton House
64 Maids Causeway
Cambridge CB5 8DD

In association with
Johnson Wax Ltd
Frimley Green
Camberley
Surrey GU16 5AJ

First published 1992
© Johnson Wax Ltd 1992

ISBN 0-85941-808-1

Design: Ken Vail Graphic Design
Photography: Steve Lee
Styling: Philomena O'Neill
Food preparation: Elizabeth Martin
Printed and bound in Great Britain by Butler & Tanner Ltd,
Frome and London

CONTENTS

Introduction

Some hard facts about Brillo

Every enthusiastic cook knows that no matter how lovingly the food is prepared, the washing-up afterwards will seem a chore – and the more elaborate and time-consuming the recipe, the higher the pile of pots and pans by the sink! However, bringing the sparkle back to cookware need not be so daunting when the tough cleaning power of Brillo is at hand.

Pots and pans may have changed in design and colour over the years, but the demand for an effective method of cleaning them still remains the same. Brillo has spent over 50 years helping you to keep cookware in tip-top condition and, as long as there are cooks, there will be a need for soap-filled scouring pads. However, Brillo also recognises the modern need for a gentler non-scratch partner to complement the traditional Brillo.

So now the soft option

BRILLO LITE is a unique non-scratch soap-filled pad developed with non-stick pans and glassware in mind, as well as lighter, healthy cooking styles and recipes. While the original Brillo will be as reliable as ever in cleaning up after the traditional family recipes loved by all, Brillo Lite accommodates the exciting change in eating attitudes and cooking techniques. Speciality cookware such as woks and microwave utensils which are used for many healthy cooking recipes need a more gentle cleaning process. Recipes which are quick to prepare and cook, the food barely touching the pan, now make 'lite' work of cleaning up!

Brillo Lite's foaming, fresh-fragranced pad is also gentle enough to use on all surfaces such as microwave ovens, cutlery, fridges and all non-stick items – and is perfect, too, for wiping around sinks, baths and paintwork.

To help you with your cleaning up, our recipes are coded by each title – purple for traditional cleaning (use Brillo original to scour your metal pans or, if using non-stick

cookware, soak in hot water before tackling with Brillo Lite); and – green for recipes which will make cleaning up a moment's work with Brillo Lite. Once again, Brillo looks set to continue its high standards of cleanliness in the changing years ahead.

THE BRILLO GUIDE TO SAUCEPANS (Choice, care and cleaning)

Saucepans and cookware were once regarded as unexciting, but essential, kitchen equipment. However, one glance around a kitchenware department will clearly illustrate that there is now a design available to suit any style of kitchen and cook! All this new equipment can be expensive, but look upon your purchase as a long-term investment; it is worth getting the best quality you can afford. And, just in case the choice is too confusing, here are a few guidelines on what to look out for and the types of saucepans available.

The right size

A set of pans usually includes a milkpan, three sizes of saucepan and a frying-pan. Before you choose them, refer to your cooking hob instructions and make a note of the sizes of the hob rings. If the pan is too small, the 'safety cut-out' (thermal limiter) may cut the heat off to prevent the hob over-heating. If there is no 'safety cut-out' the wasted heat will escape into the kitchen, causing hot working conditions while running up fuel bills. On the other hand, saucepans that are too large for the hob will not heat up or cook evenly.

The right style

● Check that the handle is comfortable to hold, well-fitted, long enough and strong enough to be safe. Solid metal handles will get hot very quickly, although many pans now have hollow metal handles which stay cool. Wooden handles are the coolest, but can become scorched if accidentally moved over a gas flame. Plastic handles are a good choice as they are heat-resistant and also dishwasher-proof.
● Feel the weight of the pan when empty, and then imagine it full of peeled potatoes. Cast-iron and copper pans can be extremely heavy.
● Check the base of the saucepan – it should be thick for good conduction of heat, flat to have the best possible contact between the heat source and the pan, and smooth to prevent scratching. Very thin, light pans are not suitable for solid hotplates or ceramic hobs.

The right material

● Good-quality **stainless steel** pans are pricey, but a good investment, as they should last you a lifetime. As stainless steel is a poor conductor of heat, a number of different materials are sandwiched into the base to improve heat conductivity.
● **Glass-ceramic** pans retain heat well, so are good for slow, even and economical cooking. They can withstand extremes of heat so can be taken straight from the fridge to the hob. Transparent glass-ceramic pans also allow you to see the food cooking without removing the lid.
● **Aluminium** is probably the most versatile and widely used material; it heats up quickly and is also quite lightweight so it is a common choice for the less able or elderly.

5

- **Cast-iron** pans are heavy, heat up slowly but retain heat well. They are good for long, slow cooking. Cast iron rusts easily so they usually have an enamel coating or a non-stick interior to protect them.
- **Copper** pans are excellent at conducting heat, but are very expensive. They will last a lifetime in the kitchen and will look wonderful if you are prepared to cherish them! They are usually lined with stainless steel, tin or aluminium.
- **Enamel** pans are made from steel, coated with enamel paint. Good-quality enamel pans are resistant to damage from heat and scratching, reasonably light, yet durable and versatile.
- **Non-stick coatings** in pans make cooking and washing-up easier. However, they need to be treated with respect, using only wooden or plastic utensils. They are a boon for sauce-making and frying and also reduce the need for additional fat in cooking.

Safety hints
- Never leave hot oil or fat unattended when frying.
- Allow your pans to cool slightly before immersing in cold water.
- Turn handles away from the edge of the cooker and other burners.
- When using a gas hob, do not let the flames flicker up and around the sides of the pan.
- To avoid spillages and boiling over, do not fill saucepans to more than two-thirds capacity. For deep-fat frying, fill the pan no more than one-third full.

Caring for your equipment
- Loosen burnt-on foods or stubborn stains by soaking in hot soapy water or a strong solution of biological washing detergent. Choose the right Brillo pad to rub away the baked-on grime – original for aluminium and steel pans and stainless steel interiors (check the manufacturers instructions if in doubt), and Lite for glass-ceramic, enamel ware and all non-stick finishes as well as the shiny outer surface of stainless steel pans.
- To remove stains in aluminium pans, boil up a weak solution of vinegar and water. Avoid soda as this will mark the pan.
- Do not leave cooked food in metal and enamel pans as salt can cause pitting of the pan surface.
- While your hob is still warm, gently wipe away any cooked-on spillages and stains with Brillo Lite.
- Grill pans, enamel baking trays and oven shelf runners soon get a build-up of grease and cooking stains. Simply clean with Brillo pads to give them back their shine.

CLEANLINESS IN THE KITCHEN

There are many areas in and around the home which provide ideal conditions for germs to breed. One of the main areas of risk is the kitchen, with its warm, moist conditions.

Adopting good food hygiene habits will help protect the family. Brillo's strong cleaning and scouring action has effectively cleaned cookware for many years, eliminating cross-contamination through dirty pots and pans. And now Brillo can help you with other cleaning jobs:

● Wipe around the sink, taps and bath with Brillo Lite before running bleach down the plug-hole.

● Use Brillo Lite to clean both the interior and exterior of microwave ovens – it will lift hard food particles and wipe away grease instantly. Finally, wipe dry with kitchen paper.

● Use Brillo Lite to clean fingerprints from cupboards, fridge doors and paintwork.

● The interior of fridges, particularly the shelves and their runners, can harbour food particles. Empty the fridge and wipe clean with Brillo Lite. Rinse and dry thoroughly.

● Both plastic and wooden chopping boards need to be kept clean. Ideally, keep one for raw and one for cooked foods. Wash wooden boards with Brillo original and plastic boards with Brillo Lite. Dry thoroughly.

● Use Brillo Lite to scour kitchen tables and work surfaces, removing stubborn particles a cloth would miss.

Tips for good hygiene
● Always wash your hands with hot soapy water before handling food.
● Keep your kitchen clean and dry; wash and dry utensils between preparation stages.
● Keep pets out of the kitchen; wash hands after touching them.
● Store raw and cooked foods separately.
● Store raw meat and poultry in covered containers in the bottom of the fridge, so they don't drip on to food that will be eaten without further cooking.
● Consume food quickly once cooked or cool rapidly and refrigerate or freeze.
● Do not keep foods beyond their 'sell by' or 'use by' dates.
● Do not reheat food more than once.
● Keep your fridge/freezer at the correct temperature. Buy a fridge thermometer.
● Use plastic pedal bins and replace the liners daily. Wash regularly.
● Disinfect your dishcloth daily. Do not use it for other jobs.
● Clean as you go.

Light Meals and Snacks

FOUR SEASONS PIZZA

Serves 4–6

BASE:	50 g (2 oz) streaky bacon rashers, chopped
250 g (8 oz) self-raising flour	50 g (2 oz) peeled prawns
1/2 teaspoon baking powder	50 g (2 oz) canned tuna, drained
50 g (2 oz) butter	50 g (2 oz) red salami, cut into strips
150 ml (1/4 pint) milk	1/2 small red pepper, chopped finely
TOPPING:	25 g (1 oz) capers
425 g (14 oz) can of chopped	1/2 small green pepper, chopped
tomatoes, drained	2 tablespoons olive oil
175 g (6 oz) mozzarella	75 g (3 oz) can of anchovies
or Cheddar cheese grated or sliced thinly	2 teaspoons dried mixed herbs
50 g (2 oz) button mushrooms, sliced	

1 Preheat the oven to Gas Mark 6/200°C/400°F. Lightly oil a flat baking sheet or pizza dish.

2 For the base, sieve the flour into a bowl with the baking powder. Rub in the butter until the mixture resembles fine breadcrumbs. Bind the mixture together with just enough milk to form a soft dough.

3 Roll out the dough on a lightly floured surface to make a 23–25 cm (9–10 inch) circle. Place on the baking sheet and cook for 10 minutes. Leave to cool. Reduce the oven temperature to Gas Mark 3/160°C/325°F.

4 Spread the chopped tomatoes over the pizza base. Sprinkle two-thirds of the cheese evenly over the top.

5 Cover one quarter of the pizza with mushrooms and bacon, another with the prawns and tuna, the next with the salami and red pepper and the last with the capers and green pepper. Drizzle on the oil, then sprinkle on the remaining cheese, strips of anchovy fillets and the mixed herbs.

6 Cook for 30–40 minutes. Serve immediately.

Cook's Hint

If you want to stock up on pizzas for the freezer, the part-baked base only will freeze for four months and a complete pizza, depending upon its topping, will freeze for 1–3 months. Defrost thoroughly before cooking. Alternatively, divide the dough into four pieces and make 15 cm (6-inch) round pizzas, each with a different topping.

Huntsman's Plait, Four Seasons Pizza

HUNTSMAN'S PLAIT

Serves 6–8

Ideal for lunchboxes or picnics, this recipe is simple to make and can be varied by trying out differently seasoned sausages and chutneys.

500 g (1 lb) puff or flaky pastry	500 g (1 lb) pork sausages,
50 g (2 oz) butter	cooked and sliced
250 g (8 oz) button mushrooms,	6 hard-boiled eggs, chopped
chopped roughly	2 tablespoons tomato chutney
1 onion, grated	1 egg, beaten
	salt and freshly ground black pepper

1 Preheat the oven to Gas Mark 6/200°C/400°F. Roll out the pastry to a 35 cm (14-inch) square on a lightly floured surface.

2 Melt the butter and lightly cook the mushrooms until all the butter has been absorbed. Remove from the heat.

3 Stir in the onion, sausages, eggs and chutney. Season to taste.

4 Spoon the filling down the centre of the pastry. Cut diagonal strips 1 cm (^{1}/2 inch) wide, each side of the filling. Take each strip separately and lay across the filling, alternating with each side. Tuck in ends to neaten.

5 Carefully transfer the plait to a dampened baking sheet, and brush it with the beaten egg.

6 Cook for 35–40 minutes, or until golden and crisp. Serve warm or cold.

Cook's Hint

Put any pastry which needs to rise well on to dampened baking sheets, e.g. puff, choux or flaky pastry. The moisture prevents the bottom of the pastry from browning too quickly and creates steam to help the pastry rise.

CURRIED EGGS

Serves 4

Serve this unusual, and more substantial, poached-egg dish with fresh crusty bread and butter. If you prefer, hard boil the eggs beforehand.

125 g (4 oz) long-grain rice	2 tablespoons lemon juice
1 small onion, chopped finely	4 eggs
25 g (1 oz) butter	2 tablespoons double cream
2 tablespoons mild curry powder	salt
15 g (^{1}/2 oz) flour	paprika for dusting
300 ml (^{1}/2 pint) chicken stock	

1 Cook the rice according to the pack instructions. Drain and keep warm.

2 Meanwhile, fry the onion in the butter until softened. Stir in the curry powder and flour and cook for a further minute.

3 Gradually blend in the stock and lemon juice, stir continuously until the sauce thickens. Simmer for 10 minutes.

4 Poach the eggs for 5–6 minutes until firm.

5 Arrange the rice in a shallow serving dish and carefully spoon the eggs on top.

6 Remove the sauce from the heat, add salt to taste, stir in the cream and pour over the eggs. Sprinkle with paprika and serve immediately.

Cook's Hint

To poach eggs successfully, place them, still in their shells, into the poaching water for 10 seconds. Then break them into a small cup and lower, carefully, into simmering water containing a teaspoon of vinegar.

SMOKED HADDOCK KEDGEREE

Serves 2 as a main course or 4 as a breakfast

250 g (8 oz) brown rice	2 tablespoons sunflower oil
2 onions, chopped finely	2 tablespoons yogurt *or* single cream
250 g (8 oz) smoked haddock fillet	2 tablespoons lemon juice
1 teaspoon hot curry paste	2 hard-boiled eggs, quartered
or 1 tablespoon medium-hot curry powder	1 tablespoon chopped fresh parsley

1 Cook the rice according to the pack instructions. Add the chopped onion for the last 15 minutes of cooking.

2 Poach the smoked haddock in just enough water to cover the base of the saucepan: bring the water to the boil, then cover the pan, switch off the heat and leave to stand for 10 minutes. Carefully drain off the cooking liquor, reserving 4 tablespoons.

3 Carefully skin the fish, remove any bones and break the flesh into bite-size pieces.

4 Drain the rice, and fold in the fish. Cover and keep warm.

5 In a small bowl, make a sauce by whisking together the fish liquor, the curry paste, or powder, sunflower oil, yogurt or cream and lemon juice. Pour this over the fish and rice.

6 Gently spoon the kedgeree into a warm serving dish, folding the sauce in at the same time. Garnish with the quartered eggs and chopped parsley.

Cook's Hint

Use canned flaked salmon for a convenient alternative or add 50 g (2 oz) peeled prawns and garnish with Dublin Bay prawns for a special occasion.

MUSHROOM STRUDEL

Serves 4–6

Individual melt-in-the-mouth parcels with a savoury mushroom and bacon filling. Make up one large strudel if you prefer, but it is trickier to divide up. Ready made frozen filo pastry is ideal for this recipe; pop the unused pastry sheets back in the freezer until required.

250 g (8 oz) streaky bacon rashers, chopped	125 g (4 oz) cream cheese, cubed
	50 g (2 oz) fresh white breadcrumbs
150 g (5 oz) butter	2 tablespoons lemon juice *or* dry sherry
1 onion, chopped finely	1 tablespoon chopped fresh parsley
2 garlic cloves, chopped finely	10–12 sheets filo pastry
500 g (1 lb) mushrooms, halved and sliced	salt and freshly ground black pepper

1 Preheat the oven to Gas Mark 6/200°C/400°F. Lightly grease a baking sheet.

2 Fry the bacon in a large saucepan, in its own fat, until cooked. Add 25 g (1 oz) of the butter, the onion and garlic and cook for a further 5 minutes until the onion is softened.

3 Stir in the mushrooms and cream cheese and cook briskly for 2 minutes or until the cheese has melted.

4 Stir in the breadcrumbs, lemon juice or sherry, and parsley. Season well with salt and pepper. Leave to cool slightly.

5 Melt the remaining butter in a small saucepan. Lay two sheets of filo pastry on top of one another on a sheet of greaseproof paper, brushing each layer liberally with melted butter. Fold in half widthways.

6 With a draining spoon, place some mushroom mixture down the middle of the pastry. Turn in the two long sides of the oblong, then moisten all the edges with water and roll up. Place the roll on the baking sheet with the seam underneath. Repeat with the remaining ingredients.

7 Brush the remaining butter over the rolls. Bake in the oven for 15–20 minutes or until the pastry is golden and crisp. Serve warm.

Cook's Hint

The thin leaves of filo pastry dry out and crack very quickly when handled. Keep the pastry covered with polythene or a damp cloth until required. Brush with butter as quickly as you can.

Mushroom Strudel, Pasticcio

PASTICCIO

Serves 4

This supper dish is good served with a salad. Although traditionally made with macaroni, you could use spaghetti and leftover roast meat can be substituted for the mince.

MEAT SAUCE:	CHEESE SAUCE:
1 onion, chopped finely	50 g (2 oz) butter
500 g (1 lb) minced beef or pork	50 g (2 oz) flour
425 g (14 oz) can chopped tomatoes	450 ml (3/4 pint) milk
2 tablespoons tomato purée	a pinch of grated nutmeg
1 teaspoon dried oregano	125 g (4 oz) Cheddar cheese, grated
1/2 teaspoon ground allspice	150 ml (5 fl oz) natural yogurt
1 garlic clove, crushed	1 egg, beaten
250 g (8 oz) macaroni	salt and freshly ground black pepper

1 Fry the onion and minced beef (or pork) together stirring until the meat is browned and the onions softened. (No cooking oil is required.)

2 Stir in the tomatoes, tomato purée, oregano, allspice and garlic. Simmer, uncovered, for 20 minutes. Season to taste with salt and pepper.

3 Preheat the oven to Gas Mark 4/180°C/350°F.

4 Bring a large pan of salted water to the boil, add the macaroni. Cook for 10 minutes until just tender. Drain.

5 Meanwhile, melt the butter in a small saucepan, add the flour and cook for 1 minute. Blend in the milk and bring to the boil, stirring vigorously until the sauce thickens.

6 Remove the pan from the heat and stir in the nutmeg, cheese, yogurt and egg. Season to taste with salt and pepper.

7 Combine the macaroni and minced beef in an ovenproof dish. Pour over the Cheese Sauce.

8 Bake in the oven for 35–40 minutes until golden brown.

Cook's Hint

When buying minced beef, look out for the leaner mince now available. There is still enough fat in it, so oil for browning is unnecessary.

LEEK & HAM GOUGÈRE

Serves 6

This delicious crisp savoury choux pastry ring is filled with a leek and ham mixture, but you can try your own combinations: replace some leek with sweetcorn kernels and mushrooms, or use cooked chicken or tuna instead of the ham.

FILLING:	1 tablespoon fresh breadcrumbs
75 g (3 oz) butter	salt and freshly ground black pepper
4 leeks, sliced	CHOUX PASTRY:
50 g (2 oz) plain flour	300 ml (½ pint) water
300 ml (½ pint) milk	125 g (4 oz) butter
150 ml (¼ pint) dry cider *or* apple juice	125 g (4 oz) plain flour, sifted
2 tomatoes, skinned, de-seeded and sliced	4 eggs, beaten
250 g (8 oz) cooked ham, cubed	75 g (3 oz) Cheddar cheese, grated

1 Preheat the oven to Gas Mark 6/200°C/400°F.

2 For the filling, melt the butter in a pan, add the leeks and fry slowly until softened. Stir in the flour and cook for 1 minute.

3 Gradually stir in the milk and cider or apple juice, and heat, stirring until thickened.

4 Add the tomatoes, ham, salt (with caution) and pepper, to taste. Cover and cool until required.

5 For the choux ring, place the water and butter in a saucepan and bring to the boil. Remove the pan from the heat and quickly beat in the flour with a pinch each of salt and pepper.

6 Cool slightly, then beat in the eggs, a little at a time. Stir in the cheese. The paste should now be smooth and glossy.

7 Spoon the choux pastry around the sides of a 1.1-litre (2-pint) shallow ovenproof dish. Spoon the filling into the centre of the choux pastry. Sprinkle with the breadcrumbs.

8 Bake in the oven for 40 minutes or until well risen and golden.

Cook's Hint

Open freeze the gougère at the end of stage **7**. Wrap in foil when it is frozen, then store for up to two months. Thaw, unwrapped, for about 3 hours at room temperature then cook.

CHICKEN & AVOCADO BAKE

Serves 4

This is a good way of using up cooked chicken – or turkey – and it also works extremely well with a mixture of cooked fish (salmon, cod or prawns). Substitute 500g (1lb) cooked broccoli florets for the avocado, if preferred. Serve with jacket potatoes and a tomato sauce.

50g (2oz) butter	500g (1lb) cooked chicken,
50g (2oz) plain flour	cut into small pieces
300ml (½ pint) milk	2 avocados, halved and skinned
150ml (¼ pint) crème fraîche	2 tablespoons lemon juice
150ml (¼ pint) chicken stock	15g (½oz) plain crisps, crumbled,
a pinch of grated nutmeg	*or* fresh breadcrumbs
	salt and freshly ground black pepper

1 Preheat the oven to Gas Mark 5/190°C/375°F.

2 Melt the butter in a saucepan. Stir in the flour and cook for 1 minute. Gradually blend in the milk, crème fraîche and stock and bring to simmering point, stirring continuously, until the sauce thickens. Cook for 2–3 minutes.

3 Season to taste with salt and pepper and add the nutmeg. Fold in the chicken.

4 Stone and quarter the avocados and slice the flesh thickly. Toss in the lemon juice. Fold into the chicken and sauce.

5 Spoon into an ovenproof casserole dish and sprinkle with the crisps or breadcrumbs. Bake for 25–30 minutes.

Cook's Hint

Crème fraîche is now widely available and is a delicious substitute for double cream – and lower in calories too! It originates from France and has a wonderful sharp flavour and a thick, creamy texture. Try it, too, spooned over fresh fruits.

Traditional Family Meals

POST-ROAST LOIN OF PORK WITH APPLE

Serves 4

This dish is an enjoyable change to the traditional family roast, and it needs little attention. For a special occasion, stir a tablespoon of Calvados into the sauce.

1 tablespoon vegetable oil	¹/₂ teaspoon dried sage
25 g (1 oz) butter	1 tablespoon plain flour
750 g (1 ¹/₂ lb) boned loin of pork, rolled and tied	375 ml (12 fl oz) chicken stock
	150 ml (¹/₄ pint) crème fraîche
2 onions, chopped finely	*or* fromage frais
2 small cooking apples, peeled, cored and sliced	salt and freshly ground black pepper

1 Preheat the oven to Gas Mark 4/180°C/350°F.

2 Heat together the oil and butter in a flameproof casserole. Fry the prepared pork all over until golden brown, then transfer to a plate.

3 Gently cook the onions in the hot oil until softened and transparent. Stir in the apple slices and sage and cook for a further 5 minutes.

4 Sprinkle the flour into the casserole and stir it into the juices. Cook for 1 minute, then gradually stir in the stock and seasoning to taste.

5 Place the loin of pork back into the casserole, spoon some apple and onion over the surface. Cover tightly and transfer to the oven to cook for 1¹/₂–2 hours, or until the pork is very tender.

6 Remove the pork, wrap in foil and leave to stand for 10 minutes.

7 Strain the juices from the casserole into a small pan. Reduce, if necessary, over a high heat before stirring in the crème fraîche or fromage frais. Adjust the seasoning to taste.

8 Serve the pork sliced, with the sauce spooned over.

Cook's Hint

If preferred, at stage 7, process together the juices, apple and onion until smooth, then whisk in the crème fraîche or fromage frais. This will give a thicker sauce – but just as delicious.

FISHERMAN'S PIE

Serves 4

Always choose fish according to what is freshly available. Try whiting, cod or coley, and for a special occasion, use a mixture of haddock and prawns. Serve with buttered carrots.

500 g (1 lb) firm white fish, skinned	3 eggs, hard-boiled and chopped
450 ml (3/4 pint) milk, plus 6 tablespoons	75 g (3 oz) frozen peas
1 bay leaf	75 g (3 oz) sweetcorn kernels
6 peppercorns	2 tablespoons chopped fresh parsley
65 g (2½ oz) butter	1 kg (2 lb) potatoes
40 g (1½ oz) plain flour	a pinch of ground nutmeg
	salt and white pepper

1 Place the fish in a saucepan with the 450 ml (3/4 pint) milk, bay leaf, peppercorns and a pinch of salt and simmer gently for 10 minutes.

2 Transfer the fish to a plate. Flake lightly and remove any bones. Strain the cooking liquor into a jug. Discard the bay leaf and peppercorns.

3 Melt 40 g (1½ oz) butter in the pan. Stir in the flour and cook over a low heat for 1 minute. Remove the pan from the heat and gradually blend in the reserved cooking liquor. Return the pan to the heat and bring to the boil, stirring continuously until the sauce thickens.

4 Stir in the chopped eggs, peas, sweetcorn and parsley. Season to taste. Fold in the flaked fish. Spoon into a 1.2-litre (2-pint) pie dish.

5 Preheat the oven to Gas Mark 6/200°C/400°F.

6 Boil the potatoes, then drain and mash them with the remaining butter and milk until smooth. Season to taste with salt, pepper and nutmeg. Spoon or pipe over the fish.

7 Bake for 30 minutes until golden brown.

Cook's Hint

For a crunchy topping, 10 minutes before the end of cooking, roughly crumble a small bag of plain salted crisps over the surface of the potato or a mixture of 50 g (2 oz) grated Cheddar cheese and 15 g (½ oz) crumbled cornflakes.

Fisherman's Pie, Chicken & Broccoli Lasagne

CHICKEN & BROCCOLI LASAGNE

Serves 4–6

Cooked turkey, ham or firm fish can be used instead of the chicken or – to transform it into a vegetable lasagne – replace the chicken with sliced courgettes, button mushrooms, whole okra and celery.

75 g (3 oz) butter	250 g (8 oz) broccoli,
1 onion, sliced thinly	blanched and cut into small pieces
75 g (3 oz) plain flour	125 g (4 oz) sweetcorn kernels
600 ml (1 pint) chicken stock	1/2 teaspoon dried mixed herbs
300 ml (1/2 pint) milk	12 sheets no-pre-cook lasagne
375 g (12 oz) cooked chicken, diced	125 g (4 oz) Cheddar cheese, grated
	salt and freshly ground black pepper

1 Preheat the oven to Gas Mark 6/200°C/400°F.

2 Melt the butter in a saucepan and fry the onion gently for 5 minutes or until softened and transparent.

3 Sprinkle in the flour and cook for a further 2 minutes, stirring frequently.

4 Remove the pan from the heat. Gradually blend in the stock and milk, stirring well. Return the pan to the heat and gradually bring to the boil stirring constantly, until the sauce thickens.

5 Remove the pan from the heat and add the chicken, broccoli, sweetcorn, herbs and seasoning to taste.

6 Spread a thin layer of sauce in the base of a 23 cm (9-inch) square ovenproof dish. Cover with four sheets of lasagne. Repeat the layers of sauce and lasagne twice more, ending with a layer of sauce.

7 Sprinkle over the cheese and bake for 35–40 minutes until golden brown and bubbling.

Cook's Hint

If cooking for one, prepare this lasagne in six individual foil containers. Sprinkle over the cheese, then freeze for up to three months. Thaw and cook as above.

MINCEMEAT COBBLER

Serves 4-6

A quick and economical family dish that just needs fresh vegetables to accompany it.

	SCONE TOPPING:
750 g (1½ lb) minced beef	
1 large onion, sliced thinly	175 g (6 oz) self-raising flour, sifted
2 carrots, diced	50 g (2 oz) butter
125 g (4 oz) button mushrooms, halved	½ teaspoon mixed dried herbs
300 ml (½ pint) beef stock	1 egg, beaten
2 tablespoons tomato chutney *or* sweet pickle	2 tablespoons milk
1 tablespoon tomato purée	½ teaspoon sesame seeds
2 teaspoons cornflour	
salt and freshly ground black pepper	

1 Preheat the oven to Gas Mark 6/200°C/400°F.

2 In a large saucepan, fry the minced beef, stirring frequently, until the juices begin to run, and the meat has browned.

3 Stir in the onion and carrots and cook for a further 2 minutes.

4 Stir in the mushrooms, stock, chutney or pickle, and tomato purée and season with salt and pepper. Gradually bring to the boil.

5 Blend the cornflour with a little cold water, and stir in to thicken. Reduce the heat and simmer for 15–20 minutes.

6 Meanwhile, make the 'cobbler' topping. Rub the fat into the flour until it resembles fine breadcrumbs. Add the mixed herbs and salt and pepper.

7 Bind together with sufficient beaten egg and milk to give a soft dough, yet firm enough to handle. Pat the dough out on to a floured surface to about 1 cm (½ inch) thick. Cut into 4 cm (1½-inch) rounds.

8 Spoon the meat into a round, shallow ovenproof dish. Place the scones in a circle, around the top of the casserole. Brush the scones with any remaining egg or milk and sprinkle on the sesame seeds.

9 Cook for 20 minutes or until the scones are well risen and golden brown.

Cook's Hint

Mix a teaspoon of mild curry powder, or 25 g (1 oz) finely grated cheese, or ½ teaspoon caraway seeds to the scone mixture as an alternative to the herbs.

SPICY BEEF & GUINNESS PIE

Serves 6

Long, slow cooking is the secret of this delicious pie, allowing the different flavours to intermingle. Accompany with creamed potatoes or parsnips and a green vegetable.

QUICK FLAKY PASTRY:	1 tablespoon sunflower oil
250 g (8 oz) plain flour	1/2 teaspoon grated nutmeg
175 g (6 oz) butter or margarine, frozen	1 large garlic clove, chopped
6 tablespoons iced water	1 kg (2 lb) lean stewing beef, cubed
1 egg, beaten	300 ml (1/2 pint) stout, e.g. Guinness
FILLING:	250 g (8 oz) no-soak prunes, pitted
1 teaspoon whole allspice berries	500 g (1 lb) carrots, sliced thickly
6 cloves	1 tablespoon cornflour
1 teaspoon juniper berries	salt and freshly ground black pepper

1 For the pastry, sieve the flour and a little salt into a bowl.

2 Wrap the end of the frozen butter or margarine in foil and coarsely grate it into the flour. Keep dipping the butter in the flour to make grating easier.

3 Add the very cold water and quickly work the mixture to form a dough that leaves the sides of the bowl clean. Wrap in foil and chill until required.

4 Preheat the oven to Gas Mark 1/140°C/275°F.

5 Crush the allspice, cloves and juniper berries with a pestle in a mortar or between 2 dessertspoons. (Alternatively, tie them in a small muslin bag.)

6 Heat the oil in a flameproof casserole dish and stir in the crushed spices, nutmeg and garlic. Cook for 1 minute.

7 Gradually add the cubes of beef, and cook over a high heat until browned all over.

8 Stir in the stout, 150 ml (1/4 pint) water and the prunes. Bring to the boil, then cover and cook in the oven for one hour. Stir in the carrots. Blend the cornflour with a little water and stir in. Cook for a further 1^1/2 hours or until the meat is tender, and the sauce thickened. Season to taste and pour the mixture into a 1.5-litre (3^1/2-pint) pie dish. Chill.

9 Preheat the oven to Gas Mark 7/220°C/425°F.

10 Roll out the pastry, on a lightly floured surface, to 5 cm (2 inches) bigger than the pie dish. Cut a 2.5 cm (1-inch) strip from the outer edge and place on the dampened rim of the dish. Brush the strip with water. Cover with the pastry lid, press lightly to seal the edges. Trim off the excess pastry and use to make pastry leaves. Glaze with the beaten egg.

11 Cook in the oven for 30–35 minutes until the pastry is golden and crisp.

Cook's Hint

Commercially produced pastry saves a lot of time and gives good results, but if you want to make your own quick flaky pastry – try the recipe above.

Spicy Beef and Guinness Pie, Barbecued Lamb Kebabs

23

BARBECUED LAMB KEBABS

Serves 4–6

Lamb leg steaks or boned noisettes can also be used for this tasty recipe. Serve on a bed of rice or with pitta bread and a tomato salad.

750 g (1 ½ lb) lean lamb	1 tablespoon olive oil
3 tablespoons tomato ketchup	1 garlic clove, crushed
2 tablespoons lemon juice	1 teaspoon Tabasco sauce
1 tablespoon clear honey	

1 Trim and cut the lamb into 2 cm (1-inch) cubes. Place in a large shallow dish.

2 Make the marinade by mixing together the tomato ketchup, lemon juice, honey, olive oil, garlic and Tabasco sauce.

3 Pour the marinade over the lamb, stirring thoroughly to coat the pieces. Cover and refrigerate for at least 2 hours.

4 Divide the meat between four skewers. Cook, under a preheated hot grill for 10 minutes, brushing with the marinade when turning. Serve immediately.

Cook's Hint

Alternate the meat with halved small tomatoes, chunks of courgette, baby sweetcorn or pieces of green pepper to 'stretch' the kebabs.

FAMILY STROGANOFF

Serves 4

The word stroganoff conjures up a picture of an elaborate meal using fillet of beef and brandy, but this trimmed-down version makes a family dish. Serve with pasta or rice.

750 g (1 ½ lb) stewing steak, cubed	300 ml (½ pint) beef stock
50 g (2 oz) plain flour	1 tablespoon tomato purée
4 tablespoons sunflower oil	2 teaspoons Worcestershire sauce
1 large onion, sliced	½ teaspoon paprika
1 garlic clove, crushed	150 ml (¼ pint) fresh soured cream
125 g (4 oz) button mushrooms,	1 tablespoon chopped fresh parsley
sliced thickly	salt and white pepper

1 Coat the meat in the flour seasoning it with salt and pepper. Heat the oil in a heavy-based saucepan and cook the meat, a few pieces at a time, until browned. Transfer to a plate.

2 Cook the onion in the remaining oil until softened. Add the garlic and the mushrooms and cook for a further 3–4 minutes.

24

3 Blend in any remaining flour, then gradually add the stock, tomato purée, Worcestershire sauce, 1 teaspoon of salt and paprika. Heat, stirring continuously, until the mixture boils and thickens.

4 Return the meat to the pan. Cover and reduce the heat to simmer slowly for 1¹/₂–2 hours or until the meat is tender.

5 Stir in the soured cream. Check the seasoning. Heat through but *DO NOT BOIL*, and transfer to a warm serving dish. Sprinkle with the chopped parsley.

Cook's Hint

To make your own soured cream, stir 2 tablespoons lemon juice into 150 ml (¹/₄ pint) double cream. Leave to stand at room temperature for 15 minutes.

CHILLI SAUSAGE CASSEROLE

Serves 4

A recipe to suit chilli and sausage fans alike – accompany it with mashed potatoes or noodles or crusty bread.

3 tablespoons vegetable oil	1 teaspoon dried oregano
500 g (1 lb) pork sausages,	2 garlic cloves, chopped
cut into 2.5 cm (1-inch) lengths	1 tablespoon tomato purée
1 large onion, chopped	425 g (14 oz) can of chopped tomatoes
1 green pepper, de-seeded and chopped	200 g (7 oz) can of red kidney beans, drained
1 tablespoon mild chilli powder	salt and pepper

1 Heat the oil in a flameproof casserole and brown the sausages on all sides. Transfer to a plate.

2 Add the chopped onion to the oil and cook gently for 5–8 minutes until transparent and softened.

3 Add the green pepper, chilli powder, oregano, garlic and 150 ml (¹/₄ pint) boiling water. Simmer for 5 minutes.

4 Stir in the tomato purée, chopped tomatoes and kidney beans. Season to taste with salt and pepper. Simmer, uncovered, for a further 5 minutes.

5 Return the sausages to the casserole, stir well, then cover and simmer for 15 minutes. Serve.

Cook's Hint

Chilli powder is made up of a blend of chilli pepper, garlic, oregano and cumin seed. If you want a 'hotter' chilli sauce, add ¹/₄ teaspoon crushed dried chillies.

Salads and Vegetables

HOT VEGETABLE & RICE SALAD

Serves 4–6

A stir-fry of mixed vegetables and rice in a Chinese-style dressing. Eat hot as a vegetable accompaniment to meat dishes or as a warm salad with cooked prawns or chicken.

375 g (12 oz) long-grain rice	50 g (2 oz) water chestnuts, sliced
2 tablespoons vegetable oil	1/2 small red pepper,
1 teaspoon sesame oil	de-seeded and sliced
1 garlic clove, chopped finely	6 button mushrooms, quartered
1 teaspoon grated fresh ginger	1 small can of bamboo shoots, drained
2 small carrots, cut into matchsticks	4 spring onions, sliced into
2 celery sticks, sliced into	1 cm (1/2-inch) diagonals
1 cm (1/2-inch) diagonals	2 tablespoons lemon juice
50 g (2 oz) green beans,	2 tablespoons Chinese wine
cut into 2 cm (1-inch) lengths	*or* dry sherry
50 g (2 oz) broccoli spears	2 tablespoons light soy sauce
50 g (2 oz) sweetcorn kernels	freshly ground black pepper

1 Cook the rice according to the pack instructions. Drain.

2 In a large pan or wok, heat the oils and fry the garlic and ginger for 2 minutes. Add the carrots, celery and beans and stir-fry over a high heat for 2 minutes.

3 Add all the remaining vegetables, except the spring onions, and stir-fry for 1 minute. (You may need a little more oil.)

4 Add the rice, toss and fry until the rice is hot. Stir in the spring onions. Remove from the heat.

5 Mix together the lemon juice, wine or sherry and soy sauce. Season with plenty of black pepper. Sprinkle over the rice mixture and stir well.

6 Spoon into a warm serving bowl and serve with extra soy sauce.

Cook's Hint

Look out for flavoured oils (Chinese chilli), sesame oil and nut oils (walnut, hazelnut, pistachio). Just a teaspoon or two tossed into stir-fried recipes, mixed into salad dressings or added to marinades can give a dish a special taste.

GARLICKY BAKED TOMATOES

Serves 4

A simple way to transform tomatoes into a tasty vegetable accompaniment.
Delicious with baked fish or cold meats and crusty bread.

500 g (1 lb) large ripe tomatoes	1 tablespoon parmesan cheese (optional)
3 garlic cloves, chopped finely	4 tablespoons olive oil
3 tablespoons white breadcrumbs	salt and freshly ground black pepper
3 tablespoons chopped fresh parsley	sprigs of fresh basil, to garnish
1 teaspoon caster sugar	

1 Preheat the oven to Gas Mark 6/200°C/400°F. Grease a shallow ovenproof dish with butter.

2 Cut the tomatoes in half and arrange them, cut side uppermost, in the dish.

3 Mix together the garlic, breadcrumbs, parsley, sugar and parmesan, if using. Season well with salt and pepper. Spoon over the tomatoes.

4 Drizzle the oil over the top and cook for 20–30 minutes or until tender. Garnish with basil and serve immediately.

Cook's Hint

Make breadcrumbs with leftover ends of brown or white bread and
store them in a rigid container in the freezer. When required, use the
breadcrumbs straight from the freezer.

MUSHROOMS & ONIONS À LA GRÈCQUE

Serves 4 as a starter or 6 as an accompaniment

This salad must be served well chilled. It can be enjoyed as a starter with hot
garlic bread, or as a salad accompaniment.

4 tablespoons olive oil	1 bay leaf, broken
12 small pickling onions	1 garlic clove, crushed
250 g (8 oz) tiny button mushrooms	2 large tomatoes, skinned and de-seeded
4 tablespoons white wine	salt and freshly ground black pepper
10 coriander seeds	2 tablespoons chopped fresh parsley, to garnish

1 Heat 2 tablespoons of the oil in a saucepan and gently cook the onions until golden and slightly softened.

2 Add the mushrooms, white wine, coriander seeds, bay leaf and garlic. Season well with the salt and pepper. Simmer, covered, for 10 minutes, shaking the pan occasionally.

3 Cut the tomatoes into thin strips and stir in. Simmer, uncovered, for a further 5 minutes. Leave to cool.

4 Remove the pieces of bay leaf. Stir in the remaining olive oil and half the parsley. Cover and chill thoroughly.

5 Serve, garnished with the remaining parsley, in a bowl as a salad accompaniment, or on individual plates, garnished with lettuce, for a starter.

Cook's Hint

If you don't have a garlic press, crush garlic with the blade of a heavy, flat knife, pressing it down hard with the heel of your hand.

Alternatively, slice the clove finely, sprinkle it with salt and then squash it with the end of a rounded knife until soft.

CARROT & APRICOT SALAD

Serves 4–6

This salad is quick to make, colourful and contains ingredients that are available all year round. Do not prepare it too far in advance or the carrots will lose some of their bulk and colour. A refreshing accompaniment to lightly spiced meat dishes and terrines.

75 g (3 oz) dried apricots, sliced thinly	1 tablespoon white wine vinegar
juice of 1 large orange	3 tablespoons olive oil
1/2 teaspoon cumin seeds	1 tablespoon chopped fresh chives
8 large carrots, grated	15 g (1/2 oz) flaked almonds, well toasted
1 small onion, grated	salt and freshly ground black pepper
1 tablespoon clear honey	

1 Soak the dried apricots in the orange juice with the cumin seeds for 20 minutes, stirring occasionally.

2 Place the grated carrot and onion in a bowl. Stir in the apricot and cumin seed mixture.

3 In a jar with a screw-top lid, shake together the honey, white wine vinegar, olive oil, chives and seasoning, to taste.

4 Toss the dressing into the carrot mixture and sprinkle the flaked almonds on top.

5 Serve slightly chilled.

Cook's Hint

Make up the dressing in advance and store in the fridge with the whole carrots and soaking apricots. The ingredients will then be well chilled when made up.

Carrot and Apricot Salad, Mushrooms and Onions à la Grècque

GREEK LEEKS

Serves 4

This dish served hot as a vegetable dish, or chilled as a salad accompaniment to cold meats, is very good whichever way you serve it.

4 leeks, cut into 2 cm (1-inch) diagonal lengths	150 ml (¼ pint) dry white wine *or* vegetable stock
½ small onion, chopped	4 tablespoons olive oil
1 garlic clove, crushed	bouquet garni
4 tomatoes, skinned, de-seeded and sliced	salt and freshly ground black pepper
	1 tablespoon chopped fresh parsley, to garnish

1 Preheat the oven to Gas Mark 4/180°C/350°F.

2 Place the leeks in an ovenproof dish, and mix in the remaining ingredients.

3 Cover tightly with foil and cook for approximately 1 hour or until the leeks are very tender.

4 Remove the bouquet garni. Adjust the seasoning and sprinkle over the parsley. Serve hot, or cool and chill until required.

Cook's Hint

To make up your own bouquet garni, tie together a small bay leaf, a spray of thyme and three or four sprigs of parsley. Alternatively place them in a small square of muslin and tie to enclose them. Vary this selection as you like depending on what other herbs are available.

PASTA SALAD NIÇOISE

Serves 4

A delicious, substantial salad, perfect to enjoy on a warm summer's day. Ideal for picnics, too! You can omit the tuna if you wish to just serve this as a side salad.

175 g (6 oz) pasta shells or spirals	1 teaspoon wholegrain mustard
250 g (8 oz) green beans	2 black olives, pitted
250 g (8 oz) tomatoes	200 g (7 oz) can of tuna chunks, drained
1 red onion, sliced thinly	1 small can of anchovy fillets,
6 tablespoons olive oil	drained (optional)
3 tablespoons lemon juice	salt and freshly ground black pepper
2 tablespoons chopped fresh basil	fresh basil leaves, to garnish

1 Cook the pasta in plenty of boiling salted water for approximately 5 minutes.

Add the green beans and cook for a further 2 minutes. Drain in a colander and rinse under cold running water. Drain. Cool, then place in a large bowl.

2 Halve or quarter the tomatoes, depending on their size. Add them and the onion to the pasta and beans.

3 Whisk together the olive oil, lemon juice, basil and mustard and add salt and pepper to taste. Gently fold the dressing into the pasta, together with the black olives.

4 Spoon into a serving bowl. Spoon the tuna into the centre of the salad. Arrange a lattice of anchovy fillets over the top, if using. Chill for 1 hour before serving. Garnish with the basil leaves.

Cook's Hint

To vary the flavour, the salad bowl can be rubbed with a cut garlic clove before putting in the salad. Add 2 stoned and chopped avocados for a touch of luxury.

RÖSTI POTATOES

Serves 4

Rösti originates from the Swiss Alps and is a delicious way to cook potatoes. Add strips of ham and crispy bacon to the potato, or grated raw carrot or celeriac. Serve, cut into wedges, as a supper dish or to accompany grilled meats.

1 kg (2 lb) potatoes, scrubbed not peeled	1 large onion, chopped finely
1 tablespoon vegetable oil	1 teaspoon salt
50 g (2 oz) butter	freshly ground black pepper

1 Boil the potatoes for 5 minutes. Drain and leave until cold. Skin the potatoes and grate coarsely into a bowl.

2 Heat together the oil and 25 g (1 oz) of the butter in a 23 cm (9-inch) frying-pan. Add the onion and cook slowly until the onion is transparent and softened.

3 Stir the onion into the grated potato. Season well with the salt and pepper.

4 Heat the remaining butter in the frying-pan and add the potato mixture. Gently pat it out into a flat cake with straight sides. Fry over a moderate heat for 10–15 minutes, pressing the rösti occasionally with a spatula.

5 When golden brown, place a large plate over the frying-pan and turn both the plate and pan over to tip the rösti on to the plate. Immediately slide it back into the pan to cook the other side for 5 minutes or until golden brown.

6 Serve hot, cut into wedges.

Cook's Hint

If you prefer to make individual rösti, use a 7 cm (3-inch) pastry cutter to shape spoonfuls of the potato mixture.

RED CABBAGE & APPLE CASSEROLE

Serves 4–6

Tangy casseroles of cabbage are popular in northern Europe. Both red and white cabbages can be used and are ideal with rich meats – roast pork, duck and pheasant. This casserole can be served chilled, too, with cold meats and pickles.

750 g (1½ lb) red cabbage	4 tablespoons red wine vinegar
2 cooking apples, peeled,	grated rind and juice of 1 orange
cored and sliced thinly	2 tablespoons port
2 onions, sliced thinly	2 tablespoons redcurrant jelly
50 g (2 oz) raisins	salt and freshly ground black pepper
2 tablespoons soft light brown sugar	

1 Preheat the oven to Gas Mark 2/150°C/300°F. Grease a deep ovenproof dish.

2 Shred the cabbage finely, removing the thick central core.

3 Put a layer of cabbage, apple and onion in the bottom of the dish. Sprinkle over some of the raisins and season well with salt and pepper.

4 In a small jug, whisk together the sugar, wine vinegar, orange rind and juice, and port. Spoon a little over the layer of vegetables. Continue layering the ingredients until they are all used up.

5 Cover and bake for 2¼–3 hours, or until the cabbage is very tender.

6 Stir in the redcurrant jelly, check the seasoning, then spoon the cabbage into a warm dish if serving it hot.

Cook's Hint

Did you know that the sour apples and wine vinegar used in this recipe help the cabbage to hold its colour? This casserole tastes even better when reheated a day or two after cooking.

Rösti Potatoes, Red Cabbage and Apple Casserole

POTATO & MUSHROOM PIE

Serves 4

A very simple, but satisfying, vegetable dish to serve on its own or as an accompaniment to grilled meat, pork chops or sausages.

1 kg (2 lb) potatoes	40 g (1½ oz) plain flour
125 g (4 oz) butter	a pinch of ground nutmeg or mace
300 ml (½ pint) milk, plus 6 tablespoons	salt and freshly ground black pepper
250 g (8 oz) button mushrooms, halved	2 tablespoons chopped fresh parsley, to garnish

1 Preheat the oven to Gas Mark 5/190°C/375°F. Lightly grease a 1.2-litre (2-pint) shallow ovenproof dish.

2 Cook the potatoes in boiling water. Drain and mash them with 50 g (2 oz) of the butter and the 6 tablespoons of milk to a smooth consistency. Season to taste.

3 Melt the remaining butter in a large pan and gently cook the mushrooms until softened. Blend in the flour and cook for a further minute.

4 Take the pan off the heat and gradually stir in the remaining milk. Return the pan to the heat and cook, stirring, until smooth and thickened.

5 Season to taste with salt, pepper and nutmeg or mace.

6 Spoon the potato mixture into a nylon piping bag fitted with a large star nozzle. Pipe a border of potato around the edge of the pie dish. Pour the mushroom mixture into the centre.

7 Cook for 15–20 minutes or until the potatoes are golden. Sprinkle with the chopped parsley and serve.

Cook's Hint

Try some of the different varieties of mushrooms now available – including the dried ones. Sprinkle 75 g (3 oz) grated cheese over the mushrooms before cooking to turn the dish into a substantial meal on its own.

BROCCOLI & COURGETTE BAKE

Serves 4–6

A recipe to make everyday vegetables more special, use cauliflower, leeks or broad beans, or a combination of potato and celeriac. This bake makes a delicious accompaniment to roast ham or chicken.

500 g (1 lb) broccoli	1/4 teaspoon ground nutmeg
3 courgettes	1 egg, beaten
50 g (2 oz) butter	25 g (1 oz) fresh white breadcrumbs
25 g (1 oz) plain flour	salt and freshly ground black pepper
300 ml (1/2 pint) milk	
(*or* 1/2 cream and 1/2 milk)	

1 Preheat the oven to Gas Mark 4/180°C/350°F. Lightly grease a 1.2-litre (2-pint) ovenproof dish.

2 Trim the broccoli and divide into florets. Slice the courgettes into 2.5 cm (1-inch) diagonal lengths.

3 Boil the broccoli in a pan of boiling water for 3 minutes, then add the courgettes and cook for a further minute. Drain, refresh in cold water. Drain thoroughly. Place in an ovenproof dish.

4 Melt 25 g (1 oz) of the butter in a saucepan, stir in the flour and cook gently for 1 minute. Remove the pan from the heat and gradually blend in the milk or milk and cream, if using. Return the pan to the heat and cook, stirring, until the sauce thickens. Simmer for 2 minutes.

5 Allow the sauce to cool slightly, then beat in the egg, nutmeg and salt and pepper, to taste. Pour over the vegetables. Sprinkle with the breadcrumbs and dot with the remaining butter.

6 Bake for 30 minutes or until set and golden. Serve.

Cook's Hint

Replace a tablespoon or two of the breadcrumbs with either grated parmesan or chopped almonds to make a change.

Puddings and Desserts

BANANA CREAM PIE

Serves 8

Very rich, and delicious, this pie can be flavoured with raspberries instead of bananas to make another version.

SHORTBREAD BASE:	CREAM FILLING:
150 g (5 oz) plain flour	1 tablespoon cornflour
1/2 teaspoon ground cinnamon	300 ml (1/2 pint) milk
75 g (3 oz) butter	150 ml (1/4 pint) single cream
40 g (1 1/2 oz) caster sugar	3 egg yolks
	25 g (1 oz) caster sugar
	1/2 teaspoon vanilla essence
	4 bananas
	TOPPING:
	175 g (6 oz) granulated sugar

1 Preheat the oven to Gas Mark 3/160°C/325°F.

2 Sift the flour and cinnamon into a bowl, add the butter and sugar and rub in until the mixture resembles fine breadcrumbs. Knead the dough until smooth.

3 Press the dough into a 20 cm (8-inch) flan dish, to cover the base evenly. Prick well all over and bake for 30 minutes until light golden and firm. Cool.

4 Make the filling: in a saucepan, blend together the cornflour and milk, bring to the boil, stirring constantly, until thickened. Cool slightly.

5 Beat in the cream, egg yolks, sugar and vanilla. Return to a very low heat and stir for 4–5 minutes until the custard thickens. *Do not boil.*

6 Peel and slice two of the bananas and scatter over the shortbread base. Pour on the warm custard, leave to cool, then chill until set (allow 2 hours).

7 Preheat the grill. Sprinkle the granulated sugar over the set custard, and heat under the grill until the sugar bubbles and caramelizes, turning very dark brown. Chill for 2 hours.

8 To serve, slice the remaining bananas and overlap them around the edge of the flan. Serve cold with single cream.

Cook's Hint

Instead of the caramel topping, omit decorating with remaining bananas and spread 150 ml (1/4 pint) whipped cream over the surface of the custard, then sprinkle with 2 crumbled chocolate flakes and a little sifted cocoa powder.

Banana Cream Pie, Iced Raspberry Yogurt

ICED RASPBERRY YOGURT

Serves 4

It is a rare occasion to enjoy a dessert that is healthy and low in calories!! This light and refreshing iced dessert can be served with tiny meringue shells or fresh fruit, such as kiwifruit or melon slices.

250 g (8 oz) raspberries, plus a few for decoration	250 g (8 oz) natural low-fat yogurt
	2 egg whites
50 g (2 oz) caster sugar	mint leaves, for decoration
1 tablespoon Crème de Cassis liqueur (optional)	

1 Gently simmer the raspberries and 25 g (1 oz) of the sugar until the fruit juices begin to run. Cool slightly, then blend or process to a purée and sieve into a freezerproof bowl.

2 Fold in the Crème de Cassis (if using) and the yogurt. Freeze for 1 hour or until just beginning to freeze around the edge.

3 Whisk together the egg whites and the remaining sugar until stiff.

4 Whisk the raspberry mixture until smooth then carefully fold in the egg white mixture. Spoon into a 900 ml (1^1/2-pint) pudding basin or oblong rigid container. Freeze for at least 3 hours, then stir through, cover and freeze for a further 3 hours.

5 To serve, turn the frozen yogurt out onto a serving plate and decorate with a few whole raspberries and fresh mint leaves. Cut into slices.

Cook's Hint

Freeze ice creams or yogurt desserts in a long narrow polythene box so they will thaw evenly and slice easily for serving.

PINEAPPLE MERINGUE SURPRISE

Serves 6

An instant pudding from the store cupboard, and a favourite with children. Serve warm with ice cream.

1 bought jam swiss roll	175 g (6 oz) caster sugar, plus extra for dusting
6 canned small pineapple rings, drained	
3 egg whites	2 glacé cherries, halved
	angelica

1 Preheat the oven to Gas Mark 7/220°C/425°F.

2 Cut the swiss roll into 7 even slices. Between each slice place a ring of pineapple (large rings should be halved). Reassemble the swiss roll onto an ovenproof serving dish.

3 Whisk together the egg whites and half the sugar, until stiff. Gradually fold in the remaining sugar. Spoon the meringue mixture over the roll shape to completely cover it. Form small swirls with a knife.

4 Bake for 7–10 minutes or until the meringue is golden and tinged with brown.

5 Decorate the meringue with the cherries and angelica and sprinkle on a little caster sugar. Serve immediately.

Cook's Hint

For a special children's occasion, make individual baked alaskas:

place a slice of swiss roll on a baking sheet, top with a pineapple ring

and a scoop of vanilla ice cream and cover with meringue. Decorate

each with cherries and angelica and cook for 2–3 minutes.

WINTER FRUIT COMPÔTE

Serves 8

A mulled fruit salad using dried and fresh fruits soaked in a lightly spiced juice is best served warm with Greek yogurt or fromage frais. Good cold too – especially for a nourishing breakfast.

125 g (4 oz) no pre-soak dried apricots	5 cm (2-inch) stick of cinnamon, halved
125 g (4 oz) no pre-soak dried prunes	150 ml (1/4 pint) orange juice
50 g (2 oz) no pre-soak dried apple pieces	6 tablespoons clear honey
50 g (2 oz) sultanas	2 pears, peeled, cored and quartered
300 ml (1/2 pint) sweet cider or cold tea	2 oranges, segmented
3 tablespoons brandy (optional)	2 bananas, sliced thickly
1 tablespoon lemon juice	12 maraschino cherries
5 cm (2-inch) piece fresh root ginger, peeled	

1 Place the dried fruits, sultanas, cider or tea, brandy (if using), lemon juice, ginger and cinnamon in a large saucepan. Gently bring to the boil, cover, then simmer for 5 minutes.

2 Stir in the orange juice, honey and pears. Simmer for a further 5 minutes. Leave to cool, remove the ginger and cinnamon, and carefully stir in the oranges, bananas and cherries.

3 Serve either warm or chilled.

Cook's Hint

If you only heat up part of the compôte, never return any hot leftovers

to the main compôte as it will spoil. Add other fruits or nuts as you

wish: frozen blackberries or toasted hazelnuts.

ALMOND TWIRLS

Makes 18

Serving home-made biscuits or wafers with a dessert adds that finishing touch to a meal. These go perfectly with the Bramble Fool (page 64), or ice creams.

250 g (8 oz) frozen puff pastry	25 g (1 oz) caster sugar
1 egg white, beaten	icing sugar or clear honey, to serve
50 g (2 oz) blanched almonds, chopped finely	

1 Preheat the oven to Gas Mark 8/230°C/450°F. Have ready two dampened baking sheets.

2 Roll out the pastry on a lightly floured surface to an oblong 30 × 20 cm (12 × 18 inches).

3 Brush half the length of pastry with egg white, then sprinkle on the nuts and caster sugar. Fold the pastry over lengthways, then roll gently, to seal together.

4 Cut into strips, twist each one, and place on the prepared baking sheets.

5 Bake for 8–10 minutes or until puffed and golden. To finish either brush with honey whilst hot, or leave to cool then dust with icing sugar. Serve freshly baked.

Cook's Hint

When accompanying gooseberry or apple fools with these twirls, add a teaspoon of ground cinnamon or mixed spice to the sugar and nuts to make a spicy biscuit.

FRENCH CHOCOLATE SPONGE

Serves 6

A light chocolate sponge covering a moist chocolate layer, this dish is very popular served warm with single cream or ice cream.

200 g (7 oz) dark chocolate	1 teaspoon vanilla essence
200 g (7 oz) butter	300 g (10 oz) plain flour
4 eggs	1 teaspoon baking powder
175 g (6 oz) caster sugar	icing sugar for dusting

1 Lightly grease a 23–5 cm (9–10-inch) ovenproof flan dish. Preheat the oven to Gas Mark 6/200°C/400°F.

2 Melt the chocolate and butter over a low heat.

3 In a bowl, beat together the eggs, sugar and vanilla essence until light and frothy. Fold in the chocolate mixture. Sift in the flour and baking powder and fold in thoroughly.

4 Pour into the flan dish and bake for 20 minutes or until risen and slightly firm to touch.

5 Dust the surface with icing sugar and serve warm.

Cook's Hint

If you own a microwave oven, save time and cook this sponge on full
power (100%) for 5 minutes and leave to stand for 5 minutes.

OLDE ENGLISH TRIFLE

Serves 6

*One of the great British puds, trifle dates back to the sixteenth century. Quite
different to the well-known tea-time trifle, this one is far more alcoholic.
Traditionally the syllabub topping was decorated with fresh primroses.*

600 ml (1 pint) milk	6 tablespoons sweet sherry
2 eggs, plus 2 egg yolks	250 g (8 oz) fresh strawberries
1 teaspoon vanilla essence	300 ml (1/2 pint) double cream
125 g (4 oz) caster sugar	4 tablespoons brandy *or* white wine
1 teaspoon cornflour	grated rind and juice of 1/2 lemon
175 g (6 oz) sponge cake	50 g (2 oz) flaked almonds, toasted
or trifle sponges	2 teaspoons icing sugar
4 tablespoons strawberry jam	

1 Heat the milk until just simmering. Meanwhile, whisk together the eggs, egg yolks,
vanilla essence, 25 g (1 oz) of the caster sugar and the cornflour. Pour on the hot milk,
whisking continuously. Return the mixture to the pan and heat gently, stirring, until the
custard thickens and coats the back of a wooden spoon. Leave to cool slightly.

2 Split the sponge cake or sponges, spread with the jam, then cut up and line
the base of a 2.5-litre (3-pint) glass dish. Sprinkle over the sherry and leave to
soak for 10 minutes.

3 Thinly slice 125 g (4 oz) of the strawberries and layer over the sponge.

4 Pour on the warm custard. Leave until cold.

5 Place the remaining caster sugar, the cream, brandy or wine, lemon juice and
rind in a bowl. Whip until the mixture is softly stiff and holds its shape. Spread over
the top of the trifle.

6 Decorate the trifle with the remaining strawberries and scatter on the flaked
almonds. Chill for 1 hour. Just before serving, lightly dust with the icing sugar.

Cook's Hint

Replace strawberries when unavailable with fresh or frozen raspberries
and replace the strawberry jam with seedless raspberry jam.

SPICED APPLE PANCAKES

Serves 4–5

Not just for Shrove Tuesday – this delicious hot pudding can be prepared well in advance and chilled or frozen until required. Try rhubarb or gooseberries instead of the apples for a change.

BATTER:	FILLING:
125 g (4 oz) plain flour	500 g (1 lb) cooking apples,
a pinch of salt	peeled, cored and sliced
1 egg	75 g (3 oz) soft brown sugar
2 tablespoons melted butter	grated rind of 1 orange
200 ml (7 fl oz) cider	50 g (2 oz) sultanas
or skimmed milk (*or* half and half)	½ teaspoon mixed spice
GLAZE:	
3 tablespoons apricot jam	
juice of 1 orange	
2 tablespoons water	
25 g (1 oz) flaked almonds	

1 Make the batter: sift the flour with the salt into a bowl. Gradually beat in the egg, melted butter and milk or cider to form a smooth batter. Heat a heavy 15 cm (6-inch) frying-pan, oil lightly and make 8–10 pancakes using 1–2 tablespoons of batter. Stack them, one on top of the other, and cover with clingfilm until required.

2 Make the filling: gently simmer the apples, sugar, orange rind, sultanas and spice for 15 minutes or until softened and pulpy.

3 Preheat the oven to Gas Mark 4/180°C/350°F. Lightly grease a shallow ovenproof dish large enough to take the pancakes folded into parcel shapes in a single layer.

4 Divide the apple filling between the centres of the pancakes and fold each pancake into a parcel shape. Place in the prepared dish.

5 Make the glaze: in a small saucepan gently heat the apricot jam, orange juice and water until smooth. Drizzle over the pancakes. Sprinkle on the flaked almonds.

6 Bake for 20–30 minutes. Serve warm with ice cream.

Cook's Hint

This enriched batter includes melted butter. Not only does this improve the flavour and colour, but it also prevents the pancakes from sticking to the pan. A tablespoon of vegetable oil also works well.

Spiced Apple Pancakes, Sticky Toffee Pudding

STICKY TOFFEE PUDDING

Serves 8–12

This calorie-laden winter pud, served with cream or custard, is perfect for Sunday lunch. If there is any left over, serve slices cold with a cup of coffee.

125 g (4 oz) butter	TOPPING:
175 g (6 oz) soft dark brown sugar	4 tablespoons double cream
4 eggs, beaten	75 g (3 oz) soft dark brown sugar
250 g (8 oz) self-raising flour	75 g (3 oz) butter
1 teaspoon bicarbonate of soda	
250 g (8 oz) stoned dates, chopped finely	
25 g (1 oz) sultanas	
2 tablespoons Camp coffee,	
or 2 teaspoons instant coffee	
300 ml (½ pint) boiling water	

1 Preheat the oven to Gas Mark 4/180°C/350°F. Grease and line a 23 cm (9-inch) square or 25 cm (10-inch) round tin. (It must be leakproof.) Prepare a foil collar to fit round the pudding later, see step 6.

2 In a bowl, cream together the butter and sugar until light and fluffy. Add the beaten eggs, a little at a time.

3 Sift in the flour and bicarbonate of soda and fold into the creamed mixture.

4 Stir in the dates and sultanas.

5 Mix together the coffee essence or instant coffee with the boiling water and pour into the mixture, which will begin to bubble. Mix thoroughly.

6 Pour into the prepared tin and bake for 1^1/2 hours or until firm to the touch and slightly shrunken in the tin. Transfer to a heatproof serving dish and fit the foil collar tightly around the sponge with a 2 cm (1-inch) rim above the top. Secure with a wooden cocktail stick.

7 Preheat the grill. Make the topping: heat the cream, sugar and butter in a small saucepan, then bring to the boil and immediately pour it over the cooked pudding.

8 Flash the pudding under the hot grill until the topping is dark and bubbling. Remove the foil collar and cocktail stick.

Cook's Hint

Keep the sponge in a warm oven at the end of stage 6 – and have the topping prepared – until required. When ready to eat the pudding, preheat the grill and proceed from stage 7. A handful of chopped walnuts or hazelnuts may be added to the pudding mixture, if liked.

RHUBARB GINGER CRUNCH

Serves 4

Rhubarb – strictly speaking a vegetable – has a relatively short season (March to June) and should not be missed. This combination of rhubarb, orange and ginger makes a perfect family pudding.

500 g (1 lb) fresh rhubarb, cut into 2.5 cm (1-inch) lengths	300 ml ($\frac{1}{2}$ pint) milk
75 g (3 oz) caster sugar	50 g (2 oz) butter
grated rind and juice of 1 orange	1 tablespoon golden syrup
1 teaspoon ground ginger	*or* orange jelly marmalade
1 egg	75 g (3 oz) rolled oats
2 tablespoons cornflour	4 gingernut biscuits, crumbled
	25 g (1 oz) almonds, chopped coarsely

1 Preheat the oven to Gas Mark 4 / 180°C / 350°F.

2 In a large saucepan, gently cook the rhubarb with 50 g (2 oz) of the caster sugar, the orange rind and juice, and ginger until just tender. Spoon into a 600 ml (1-pint) ovenproof dish.

3 In a large measuring jug, whisk together the egg, cornflour and remaining sugar.

4 Heat the milk in a small saucepan until just simmering. Quickly whisk into the egg mixture. Rinse out the saucepan and return the custard to the pan, stirring continuously over a low heat until thickened and smooth. Pour over the rhubarb. Leave to cool.

5 Melt the butter and syrup or marmalade together in a pan and stir in the oats, crumbled gingernuts and almonds. Sprinkle over the top of the custard.

6 Bake for 30 minutes. Serve warm or cold.

Cook's Hint

For a more luxurious custard sauce, replace the whole egg with 2 egg yolks. The sauce will be richer in flavour and colour and will have a thicker consistency. The spare egg whites can be used to make a meringue topping as a change from the oat and nut one.

Cakes and Bakes

LEMON & SULTANA SHORTBREAD

Makes 6–8 pieces

If these buttery fingers last long enough, they will store in an airtight container for a week. They are ideal to enjoy with mid-morning coffee.

50 g (2 oz) caster sugar,	175 g (6 oz) plain flour
plus extra for dredging	75 g (3 oz) sultanas
125 g (4 oz) butter	25 g (1 oz) mixed peel
finely grated rind of 1 small lemon	

1 Preheat the oven to Gas Mark 6/200°C/400°F. Lightly grease an 18 cm (7-inch), shallow, square or round tin.

2 Cream together the sugar, butter and lemon rind until light and fluffy.

3 Gradually add the flour, mixing well after each addition. Stir in the sultanas and mixed peel.

4 Knead the mixture to form a smooth dough. Press into the tin.

5 Bake for 25 minutes until golden brown. Mark into 6–8 pieces while still hot. Cool in the tin. Dredge with caster sugar.

Cook's Hint

Try other flavourings for this shortbread – add a pinch of mixed spice and currants, or chopped dried apricots and orange peel. A teaspoon of dried mint is also very good.

CHOCOLATE TRUFFLE CAKE

Makes 12 slices

A classic chocolate cake that is beautifully moist and is for those special indulgent moments!

For the cake:	For the syrup:
200 g (7 oz) soft light brown sugar	50 g (2 oz) granulated sugar
200 g (7 oz) plain flour	5 tablespoons water
40 g (1¹/₂ oz) cocoa powder	For the frosting:
1 tablespoon baking powder	300 ml (¹/₂ pint) double cream
1 teaspoon salt	275 g (9 oz) dark chocolate
4 eggs, separated	125 g (4 oz) unsalted butter
125 ml (4 fl oz) milk	1 tablespoon cocoa powder
125 ml (4 fl oz) sunflower oil	

Chocolate Truffle Cake, Lemon and Sultana Shortbread

1 Preheat the oven to Gas Mark 4/180°C/350°F. Lightly grease and line a 23 cm (9-inch), round, loose-based cake tin.

2 In a large bowl, mix together all the dry ingredients.

3 Beat in the egg yolks, milk and sunflower oil to form a smooth batter.

4 Whisk the egg whites until they form good peaks but are not too dry. Gently fold into the batter.

5 Pour the mixture into the prepared cake tin and bake for 50–60 minutes or until nicely risen and cooked through. Test with a warm skewer. Leave in the tin to cool.

6 Make the syrup: dissolve the sugar in the water in a small pan. Bring the syrup to the boil for 2–3 minutes. Remove the pan from the heat. Skewer the cake all over, and then pour on the hot syrup. Leave until completely cold – preferably overnight.

7 For the filling: gently heat the cream, chocolate and butter in a saucepan, stirring continuously until the chocolate has melted. Remove the pan from the heat and pour into a bowl to cool. Do not stir.

8 When cold, whisk the mixture until it forms soft peaks. Sandwich and cover the chocolate cake with the filling. Dust with the cocoa powder. Chill well before serving.

Cook's Hint

If you wish, replace 2 tablespoons of the water for the syrup with dark rum or brandy.

TREACLE CRUNCHIES

Makes 20

Very moreish and quick to make. The coconut can be replaced with ground almonds for a different flavour.

125 g (4 oz) self-raising flour	150 g (5 oz) caster sugar
75 g (3 oz) rolled oats	2 tablespoons treacle
25 g (1 oz) desiccated coconut	1 teaspoon bicarbonate of soda
125 g (4 oz) butter	1 tablespoon milk

1 In a bowl, mix together the flour, oats and coconut.

2 Heat together the butter, sugar and treacle until melted. Stir into the dry ingredients.

3 Dissolve the bicarbonate of soda in the milk and stir into the mixture. Chill for 30 minutes.

4 Preheat the oven to Gas Mark 5/190°C/375°F. Lightly grease three large baking sheets.

5 Roll the mixture into 20 small balls and place well apart on the baking sheets.

6 Bake for 12–15 minutes. Allow to cool for 2 minutes before using a spatula to transfer the crunchies to a wire rack.

7 Store in an airtight container.

Cook's Hint

This recipe works well in the microwave oven, although they end up looking like brandy snaps! Place 3 at a time on parchment paper and cook on full power (100%) for 1 minute until well spread and lacy in appearance. Cool on paper.

WELSH CAKES

Makes about 14

Freshly baked on a griddle or bakestone set above the hearth, these cakes were traditionally served at Welsh inns to weary travellers. They must be served fresh, preferably warm from the griddle, sprinkled with caster sugar and a knob of butter.

250 g (8 oz) self-raising flour	75 g (3 oz) currants
50 g (2 oz) lard	a pinch of ground nutmeg
25 g (1 oz) butter	1 egg, beaten
50 g (2 oz) caster sugar, plus extra for dusting	plain flour for dusting

1 Sieve the flour into the bowl. Rub in the lard and butter until the mixture resembles fine breadcrumbs.

2 Stir in the sugar, currants and nutmeg. Add the beaten egg and enough cold water to mix to a soft dough.

3 Press out onto a floured board to a thickness of 1–2 cm ($^1/_4$–$^1/_2$ inch) and cut into 5 cm (2-inch) rounds.

4 Dust a thick frying-pan or griddle with flour, heat, then cook the cakes on one side for approximately 4 minutes or until golden brown. Turn over and continue cooking until the second side is golden brown.

5 Transfer the cakes to a wire rack and dust with caster sugar. Serve warm, or cooled but still very fresh, buttered.

Cook's Hint

Add $^1/_2$ teaspoon mixed spice or the grated rind of $^1/_2$ lemon and sultanas may be added for flavour instead of the currants.

ORANGE DRIZZLE CAKE

Serves 8

This moist cake can be flavoured with lemon or a combination of orange and lemon.

125 g (4 oz) butter	2 tablespoons milk
125 g (4 oz) caster sugar	SYRUP:
grated rind of 1 large orange	juice of 1 large orange
2 eggs	125 g (4 oz) icing sugar,
175 g (6 oz) self-raising flour	plus extra for decoration
a pinch of salt	

1 Lightly grease and line a 20 cm (8-inch) cake tin. Preheat the oven to Gas Mark 4/180°C/350°F.

2 In a bowl, cream together the butter and sugar until light and fluffy. Beat in the orange rind and gradually beat in the eggs.

3 Sieve the flour and salt together and fold into the creamed mixture, adding some milk, if necessary, to form a soft dropping consistency.

4 Spoon the mixture into the prepared tin and bake for 30 minutes or until springy to the touch and golden. Loosen, but leave in the tin.

5 To make the syrup, gently heat the orange juice and icing sugar until dissolved. Prick the cake all over with a skewer or fine-pointed knife and saturate the cake with the hot syrup.

6 Leave till cold, then remove the cake from the tin and dust heavily with icing sugar. Store in an airtight container.

Cook's Hint

With the addition of 1 teaspoon of baking powder, this cake can be made by the all-in-one method: simply place all the ingredients in a bowl or food processor and mix together till smooth.

Banana Fruit Loaf, Orange Drizzle Cake

BANANA FRUIT LOAF

Makes 10–12 slices

This is the perfect way to use up those over-ripe black bananas. The loaf improves with keeping and freezes well.

75 g (3 oz) butter	¹/₂ teaspoon salt
175 g (6 oz) caster sugar	¹/₂ teaspoon mixed spice
2 eggs, beaten	125 g (4 oz) canned pineapple pieces,
500 g (1 lb) very ripe bananas, mashed	drained and chopped
250 g (8 oz) self-raising flour	125 g (4 oz) sultanas
¹/₂ teaspoon bicarbonate of soda	50 g (2 oz) glacé cherries

1 Preheat the oven to Gas Mark 4/180°C/350°F. Grease a 1 kg (2 lb) loaf tin.

2 Cream the butter and sugar until pale and fluffy, then beat in the eggs, a little at a time. Add the mashed bananas, mixing thoroughly.

3 Sift in the flour, bicarbonate of soda, salt and spice, and gently fold in together with the pineapple pieces, sultanas and glacé cherries.

4 Spoon into the prepared tin and cook for 1 ¹/₄ hours or until well risen and firm. Turn out and cool on a wire rack.

5 Store for 24 hours before serving, sliced and buttered.

Cook's Hint

Replace 75 g (3 oz) of the fruit mixture with chopped walnuts or hazelnuts. Drizzle a lemon glacé icing over the surface of the loaf (mix 75 g (3 oz) icing sugar with the lemon juice) to turn it into a tea-time 'cake'.

PEANUT FLAPJACKS

Makes 16

Flapjacks can vary so much – but the basic ingredients should always include butter (not margarine), sugar and rolled oats. Try soft light brown sugar instead of caster, for a richer darker bake – and you could use coconut instead of peanuts.

250 g (8 oz) butter	¹/₂ teaspoon allspice
2 tablespoons golden syrup	175 g (6 oz) plain flour
300 g (10 oz) caster sugar	¹/₂ teaspoon bicarbonate of soda
125 g (4 oz) rolled oats	1 teaspoon vanilla essence
125 g (4 oz) salted peanuts, chopped finely	

1 Preheat the oven to Gas Mark 5/190°C/375°F. Lightly grease and line the base of a 33 × 23 cm (13 × 9 inch) swiss roll tin.

2 Melt the butter and syrup in a large saucepan.

3 Add the remaining ingredients and mix together thoroughly.

4 Press the mixture into the prepared tin and bake for 35–40 minutes.

5 Leave to cool for 10 minutes before cutting into fingers. Once cold, transfer from the tin and store in an airtight container.

Cook's Hint

When measuring out syrup or treacle, rinse measuring spoons in very hot water so that the syrup will slip off easily without too much waste.

One tablespoon holds approximately 25 g (1 oz) by weight.

TRADITIONAL TEA LOAF

Makes 10 slices

This loaf needs to be prepared the day before cooking and is best served a few days after baking. It's worth waiting for!

250 g (8 oz) mixed dried fruit	1 egg
250 g (8 oz) soft dark brown sugar	300 g (10 oz) self-raising flour
300 ml (½ pint) strong cold tea	

1 Soak the fruit and sugar in the tea in a bowl overnight.

2 Preheat the oven to Gas Mark 3/160°C/325°F. Lightly grease and line a 500 g (1 lb) loaf tin.

3 Beat the egg into the fruit mixture, then fold in the sieved flour. Pour into the prepared tin.

4 Bake in the oven for 1½ hours. Leave to cool, then store in an airtight container.

5 Slice thinly and serve buttered.

Cook's Hint

Replace 50 g (2 oz) of the mixed dried fruit with chopped dates or walnuts. Add a teaspoon of mixed spice.

Special Menus

Menu 1

Warm Seafood Salad

Pheasant with Grapes, Potato Boulangère

Orange Meringue Bombe, Chocolate Sauce

WARM SEAFOOD SALAD

Serves 4 as a starter or 2 as a main course.

Choose the best and freshest fish available. Large prawns and salmon are good or, as in this recipe, monkfish and scallops. The combination of fish, smoked bacon and fresh toasted pine kernels works well together. Serve as a starter or for a light lunch, accompanied with fresh wholemeal bread.

250g (8oz) monkfish	½ teaspoon french mustard
4 large scallops	selection of salad leaves, e.g. frisée,
4 streaky smoked bacon rashers, de-rinded	radicchio, lamb's lettuce
25g (1oz) pine kernels	salt and freshly ground black pepper
4 tablespoons olive oil	TO GARNISH:
1 tablespoon white wine vinegar	1 lemon, cut into eight
1 tablespoon lemon juice	sprigs of fresh chervil

1 Wash and dry the fish. Cut the monkfish into 2.5 cm (1-inch) medallions. Detach the pink corals from the scallops. Cut the scallops in half across the centre.

2 In a non-stick frying-pan, fry the bacon in its own fat until brown and crispy. Add the pine kernels and fry until golden. Transfer the mixture to a plate and reserve. Wipe out the frying-pan with kitchen paper.

3 Mix together 3 tablespoons olive oil, the wine vinegar, lemon juice, mustard and salt and pepper to taste.

4 Wash and drain the salad leaves. Tear into bite-sized pieces and toss in a bowl together with the dressing. Divide between four serving plates.

5 Heat the remaining olive oil in the frying-pan and cook the monkfish for 3–4 minutes or until it turns from opaque to white. Divide between the four plates of lettuce.

6 Fry the scallops and corals for a minute on each side. Add to the monkfish.

7 Return the bacon and pine kernels to the frying-pan and cook briskly for 1 minute to warm through. Sprinkle evenly over the fish.

8 Garnish with the lemon wedges and fresh chervil.

Cook's Hint

For a more substantial lunch, mix chopped avocado into the salad leaves.

Look out for the more reasonably-priced 'queenies' – a smaller version of the scallop and just as good.

PHEASANT WITH GRAPES

Serves 4–6

Use the plumper, more succulent, hen pheasant for this delicate recipe. One pheasant will serve two or three people.

2 tablespoons butter	200 ml (7 fl oz) dry white wine
2 tablespoons vegetable oil	1 tablespoon redcurrant jelly
2 plump hen pheasants	200 ml (7 fl oz) crème fraîche
1 small onion	125 g (4 oz) black or red grapes,
1 carrot, halved	de-seeded and halved
1 bay leaf	salt and freshly ground black pepper
150 ml (1/4 pint) good chicken stock	

1 Heat the butter and oil together in a large flameproof casserole. Brown the pheasants all over for about 15 minutes. (You may find it easier to do one at a time.)

2 Add the onion, carrot, bay leaf and season well with salt and pepper. Pour on the stock and wine.

3 Cover tightly and cook over a low heat for 1–1^{1}/4 hours or until the pheasants are tender. (Turn the pheasants over half-way through cooking.)

4 Remove the pheasants, skin and, easing the breast meat away from the bone, neatly join them. Keep warm.

5 Boil the juices in the casserole down by half. Strain into a jug discarding the vegetables and bay leaf. Return the juices to the casserole and stir in the redcurrant jelly.

6 At this stage, if necessary, return the jointed pheasant to the casserole, cover tightly and keep warm over a very low heat until required.

7 When ready to serve, transfer the pheasant to a shallow serving dish. Stir the crème fraîche into the juices with the grapes. Bring to the boil, then reduce the heat. Adjust the seasoning, to taste.

8 Spoon the sauce and grapes over the pheasant and serve with boulangère potatoes and fresh vegetables.

Cook's Hint

Guinea fowl, poussin or chicken breasts all work well in this recipe, but reduce the cooking time accordingly.

Replace the white wine and grapes with claret and 12 soaked prunes for a more robust but equally delicious sauce.

BOULANGÈRE POTATOES

Serves 4–6

Ideal for entertaining, this dish will keep in a warm oven for some time without spoiling.

50 g (2 oz) butter, melted	3 tablespoons fresh white breadcrumbs
750 g (1½ lb) potatoes, sliced thinly	salt and freshly ground black pepper
2 onions, sliced thinly	1 tablespoon chopped fresh parsley
a pinch of ground nutmeg	for garnishing
200 ml (7 fl oz) vegetable stock	

1 Preheat the oven to Gas Mark 4/180°C/350°F. Brush the base and sides of a large, shallow ovenproof dish with half of the melted butter.

2 Arrange the potatoes and onions in layers, seasoning with a little salt, pepper and nutmeg as you go.

3 End with a layer of potatoes in overlapping slices.

4 Pour in the stock and drizzle on the remaining butter. Cook for one hour then sprinkle over the breadcrumbs and cook for a further $1/2$ hour or until the potatoes are tender and the surface browned.

5 Sprinkle the parsley over the potatoes. Serve hot.

Cook's Hint

Store fresh breadcrumbs, chopped parsley or grated cheese in the

freezer, in a rigid container, and just take out what you require.

ORANGE MERINGUE BOMBE

Serves 6–8

This special dessert can be served straight from the freezer as the liqueur prevents it from freezing solid. A good recipe for using up broken meringue shells!

4 egg whites	2 tablespoons orange liqueur
250 g (8 oz) caster sugar	e.g. Grand Marnier
450 ml (3/4 pint) double cream	grated rind and juice of 2 oranges

1 Preheat the oven to Gas Mark $1/2$/130°C/250°F. Line baking sheets with waxed paper.

2 In a bowl, whisk the egg whites until stiff and very dry. Whisk in half the sugar and then fold in the remainder a tablespoon at a time.

3 Drop spoonfuls of the mixture onto the lined baking sheets and bake for approximately 2 hours until dry and lightly coloured. Cool on a wire rack.

4 Whip the cream until thick, fold in the liqueur and the grated orange rind and juice.

5 Break the meringues into small pieces and fold into the cream.

6 Transfer the meringue mixture into a rigid covered container and freeze for 3 hours or until required.

7 Serve small scoopfuls with chocolate sauce and crisp biscuits, e.g. brandy snaps.

Cook's Hint

When baked meringues are cooked and dry right through, they will lift off the lined baking sheet very easily.

CHOCOLATE SAUCE

Serves 6–8

This is a rich sauce which will keep well in the fridge for up to two weeks. Serve only small portions!

175 g (6 oz) plain chocolate, e.g. Bournville	2 tablespoons golden syrup
	50 g (2 oz) butter
4 tablespoons water	1 teaspoon vanilla essence

1 Melt the chocolate in a bowl set over a pan of simmering water.

2 Stir in the water, syrup, butter and vanilla essence and heat gently until the sauce is thin and glossy. Serve warm. To store, pour into a screw-top jar or bowl (and cover) and keep in the fridge.

Cook's Hint

For a more economical sauce, replace the chocolate with 3 tablespoons each of cocoa powder and granulated sugar. A teaspoon of instant coffee can replace the vanilla essence to make a mocha flavour.

Menu 2

Tomato, Avocado and Mozzarella Salad

Crusty Herb and Garlic Bread

Armenian Lamb and Rice Pilau

Bramble Fool and Almond Twirls (page 40)

TOMATO, AVOCADO & MOZZARELLA SALAD

Serves 4

A delicious Italian salad, simple, fresh and colourful. Do use fresh basil – there really is no substitute.

6 tablespoons olive oil	1 ripe avocado
2 tablespoons lemon juice	salt and freshly ground black pepper
2 tablespoons chopped fresh basil	To GARNISH:
6 ripe tomatoes, sliced thinly	8 pitted black olives
250 g (8 oz) mozzarella cheese, sliced thinly	fresh basil leaves

1 Prepare the dressing: put the olive oil, lemon juice, fresh basil and salt and pepper in a jar with a screw-top lid. Shake vigorously. (The dressing can be chilled at this stage.)

2 Arrange the tomato slices and mozzarella slices alternately on one side of individual plates.

3 Cut the avocado in half and twist to remove the stone. Peel off the skin, then slice the flesh lengthways. Place a quarter of the avocado on each plate, then fan open the slices by pressing down gently.

4 Pour the chilled dressing over the avocado and tomato. Garnish with the olives and a sprig of fresh basil. Serve.

Cook's Hint

If saving half an avocado till the next day, leave the stone in place, wrap in clingfilm and then foil and refrigerate. A ripe banana wrapped in a brown paper bag with an under-ripe avocado will make it ripen more quickly.

CRUSTY HERB & GARLIC BREAD

Serves 4–6

No matter how much you make, there never seems to be enough! You can prepare garlic bread a day in advance and keep it refrigerated until it is required. Better still, keep a batch in the freezer.

1 crusty stick of french bread	1 teaspoon mixed dried herbs
2 garlic cloves, crushed	75 g (3 oz) butter
25 g (1 oz) fresh parsley, chopped finely	

1 Preheat the oven to Gas Mark 6/200°C/400°F.

2 Slice the bread diagonally three-quarters of the way through at 5 cm (2-inch) intervals.

3 In a small bowl, use a fork to blend together the garlic, parsley, dried herbs and butter with 2 teaspoons hot water. Spread this mixture on both sides of the cut slices.

4 Wrap the bread loosely in foil and bake for 20 minutes. Serve hot.

Cook's Hint

Try 1 teaspoon mild curry powder as a flavouring instead of dried
herbs. For a softer hot loaf, use a Vienna loaf or a plaited milk loaf.
The inside stays soft while the outside goes beautifully crisp.

ARMENIAN LAMB

Serves 4

*A lightly spiced dish that does not mind waiting for late guests! Accompany it with
plain green beans or the carrot and apricot salad (page 28) and pilau rice (below).*

750 g–1 kg (1½–2 lb)	1 teaspoon ground cumin
fillet end leg of lamb	1 teaspoon ground allspice
1 tablespoon sunflower oil	2 tablespoons tomato purée
25 g (1 oz) butter	300 ml (½ pint) beef stock
2 onions, sliced	salt and freshly ground black pepper
1 garlic clove, chopped	leaves/sprigs of fresh coriander
25 g (1 oz) plain flour	*or* flat-leafed parsley, to garnish

1 Remove the bone from the meat and cut the flesh into 2 cm (1-inch) squares.

2 Heat the oil and butter in a pan, and fry the meat – a few pieces at a time –
until brown.

3 Remove the meat from the pan, add the onions and garlic and cook for 5 minutes.

4 Sprinkle in the flour and spices, and cook for a further 3–4 minutes.

5 Gradually blend in the tomato purée and the stock and stir continuously until
the mixture boils and thickens.

6 Reduce the heat and add the meat. Cover and simmer for 1–1½ hours until
the meat is tender. Stir occasionally.

7 Transfer the meat to a serving dish and keep warm. Bring the sauce to the boil
and cook for a minute or two to reduce and thicken it slightly. Season to taste and
pour over the meat.

8 Garnish with fresh coriander or parsley, and serve with Pilau Rice (below).

PILAU RICE

20 g (¾ oz) butter	40 g (1½ oz) currants
1 small onion, chopped finely	½ small green pepper,
175 g (6 oz) long-grain rice	de-seeded and chopped
350 ml (12 fl oz) chicken stock	15 g (½ oz) flaked almonds, toasted

1 Melt the butter in a saucepan and add the onion and cook till golden brown. Stir in the rice and cook for a further 2–3 minutes.

2 Add the stock and bring to the boil. Reduce the heat, cover and simmer for 10 minutes.

3 Stir in the currants and chopped pepper, cover and continue cooking for 5 minutes until the stock is completely absorbed and the rice is tender.

4 Tip into a serving dish or spoon at either end of the lamb, fluff up with a fork and sprinkle over the toasted almonds.

Cook's Hint

To keep rice warm for 10 minutes or so, put it in a bowl placed over a saucepan of barely simmering water. Cover the bowl with a clean tea towel. (A microwave oven reheats rice superbly in just a few minutes.)

BRAMBLE FOOL

Serves 4

An old-fashioned dessert, fresh tasting and easy to make. Serve with fingers of shortbread or Almond Twirls (page 40).

500 g (1 lb) blackberries	2 tablespoons crème de cassis (optional)
125 g (4 oz) caster sugar	300 ml (1/2 pint) double cream
4 tablespoons water	

1 Put the blackberries, sugar and water in a saucepan. Cover and cook gently for 20 minutes or until soft and pulpy. Rub through a nylon strainer and allow to cool. Stir in the crème de cassis, if using.

2 Lightly whip the cream until if forms soft peaks. (If it is too thick it will not fold into the purée smoothly.) Fold all but 6 tablespoons of the blackberry purée into the cream.

3 Spoon the mixture into four tulip-shaped wine glasses. Chill thoroughly for 2 hours.

4 Carefully spoon the remaining purée over the surface of each fool, to form a blackberry glaze. Serve.

Cook's Hint

Greek yogurt or crème fraîche can replace the double cream, but you may need to add more sugar.

Try other fruits when they are in season – raspberries, redcurrants, rhubarb or gooseberries.